Meet the ELEPHANT

Susanna Keller

PowerKiDS press

New York

Published in 2010 by The Rosen Publishing Group, Inc.
29 East 21st Street, New York, NY 10010

First Edition

Editor: Amelie von Zumbusch
Book Design: Kate Laczynski
Photo Researcher: Jessica Gerweck

Photo Credits: Cover, pp. 1, 6, 8, 10, 14, 16, 18, 20, 22, 24 (calf, plants, trunk) Shutterstock.com; p. 4 © www.istockphoto.com/Abas Kamal bin Sulaiman; pp. 12, 24 (wrinkled) © www.istockphoto.com/TextPhoto.

Library of Congress Cataloging-in-Publication Data

Keller, Susanna.
  Meet the elephant / Susanna Keller. — 1st ed.
      p. cm. — (At the zoo)
  Includes index.
  ISBN 978-1-4358-9312-2 (library binding) — ISBN 978-1-4358-9736-6 (pbk.) — ISBN 978-1-4358-9737-3 (6-pack)
  1. Elephants—Juvenile literature. I. Title.
  QL737.P98K45 2010
  599.67—dc22

                                                           2009022250

Manufactured in the United States of America

CPSIA Compliance Information: Batch #WW10PK: For Further Information contact Rosen Publishing, New York, New York at 1-800-237-9932

CONTENTS

Huge Animals 5

African or Asian? 13

Wonderful Trunks 17

Words to Know 24

Index 24

Web Sites 24

Have you ever seen an elephant at a zoo? These animals are both big and smart.

Elephants are huge! In fact, they are Earth's largest living land animals.

Even baby elephants are big. Newborn **calves** can weigh more than 200 pounds (91 kg)!

Mother elephants take good care of their babies. They teach the calves many things.

12

This elephant is an African elephant. African elephants have very big ears and **wrinkled** skin.

14

Asian elephants are a bit smaller than African elephants. Asian elephants have smaller ears, too.

16

All elephants have long noses, called **trunks**. Elephants use their trunks to pick things up.

Elephants touch each other with their trunks. This is how they welcome friends.

To drink, elephants draw water into their trunks. Then, they spray it into their mouths.

Elephants eat **plants**. They use their trunks to bring food to their mouths.

WORDS TO KNOW

calf

plants

trunk

wrinkled

INDEX

WEB SITES

C
calves, 9, 11

E
ears, 13, 15

M
mouths, 21, 23

T
trunks, 17, 19, 21, 23

Due to the changing nature of Internet links, PowerKids Press has developed an online list of Web sites related to the subject of this book. This site is updated regularly. Please use this link to access the list: www.powerkidslinks.com/atzoo/eleph/